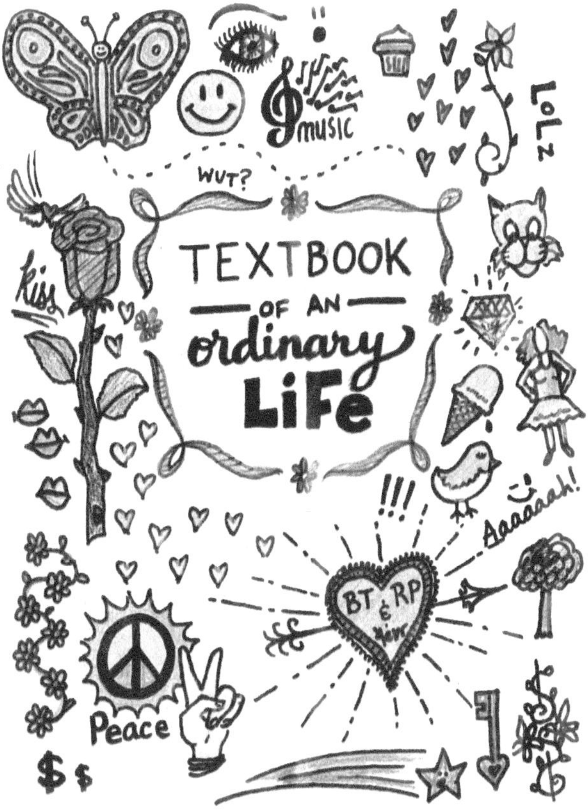

Textbook of an Ordinary Life

– Poems –

Rachel Toalson

Other Books by Rachel

Poetry

This is How You Know
Life: a definition of terms
The Book of Uncommon Hours: haiku poetry

Essay

Parenthood: Has Anyone Seen My Sanity?
The Life-Changing Madness of Tidying Up After Children
This Life With Boys
We Count it All Joy: Essays
Hills I'll Probably Lie Down On

To see all the books Rachel has written, please click or visit the link below:

www.racheltoalson.com/writing

Rachel Toalson

- Poems -

Batlee Press
PO Box 591596
San Antonio, TX 78259

Copyright ©2018 by Rachel Toalson
All rights reserved.

No part of this book may be reproduced or transmitted in any form or by any means, electronic or mechanical, including photocopying and recording, or by any information storage and retrieval system, without permission in writing. For information, address Batlee Press, PO Box 591596, San Antonio, TX 78259.

The author appreciates your taking the time to read her work. Please consider leaving a review wherever you bought it, or telling your friends how much you enjoyed it. Both of those help get the book into the hands of new readers, which is incredibly important for authors. Thank you for your support.
www.racheltoalson.com

Manufactured in the United States of America

First Edition—2018/Cover designed by Toalson Marketing
www.toalsonmarketing.com

*To my mom, who loved me
and to my dad, who left me
and to all the ones
who have been loved and left
which is to say:
all of us*

Introduction

Life is a collection of compartments: our romantic moments, our mundane tasks, our business pursuits, our random musings and wonderings. Over the course of a year, as I pen my daily poetry, I find that I write about many different subjects—my family, my writing, my hopes and dreams, my past. All of these are all of me. I cannot write one without the other.

The wide variety of subjects about which I write made it relatively simple to collect them into a textbook of sorts, spanning the heights and depths of life. As I considered these things that make me who I am, I could feel myself grow stronger, taller, more. I am not a lone entity; I am the sum of many parts.

We are the sum of our experiences—the past, the present, the future—and we are never, at any moment, a simple organism defined by a single moment in time. We are textbooks of our own lives. We are testaments to persistence, love, and the ever-present hope that is a hallmark of humanity.

We are not a single mistake; we are a thousand victories as well. We are not defined by that dark moment in our past; we are defined by how we fell to the bottom of the world and got back up. We are not abandoned, isolated, unworthy; we are the brave, the brilliant, the worthy.

We are one part of the whole of humanity. And that is something extraordinary.

Tracks

I walked along the
railroad tracks today
where my brother and sister and I
used to spend
our afternoons as kids.
I sat on the rails,
felt their cold gnaw
through my jeans,
watched the rain,
listened to my children wonder,
from the car, at the
newness of an experience:
this abandoned train track
that held pieces of
their mother's childhood.

And it all sounded
like poetry to me.

Story

It's hard to say what inspires.
Sometimes it is the gentle light
of a morning, a pale glowing
in the east that makes the fog
in the air, left over
from the night,
shimmer.

Sometimes it is the curve
of a tiny cheek, turned toward
the sleepy light,
marked with fluttering lashes.

Sometimes it is a word,
a picture, wisdom someone
shared a hundred years ago.

They all open
the cascade of creativity,
marrying a pen to a page
so another story is born.

The Idea

What is this that
wakes me from sleep
when little ones lie
peacefully across the hall?

An idea, singular,
a snippet, a thread,
and as I rise, shaking off the covers,
it is gone like the years.

Here they come to
knock and pile and kick and twist
and the losing, the tearing away,
settles into a brow

So that even when food is given,
smiles are shared, love lifts
the top of a wooden table,
it is there, a great hole of nothing

Nagging, stealing, splashing light with gray,
turning a head from what is before
and around and all in between

so the happy day smudges at the edges.

It is work and pain
and pleasure and despair,
love and hate,
a relentless torture, this art.

And yet
it is life for
the ones it calls
who dare to dance.

Lovely Dissection

When I read a good book,
I feel torn, shredded, unwrapped.
Every part of me,
every secret,
every longing exposed,
those words melting into me
like they are liquid wisdom,
come to bid me stay a while and think.
The mind meditates on the words read,
and it's important for those words
to say something good and true,
something that challenges
who we have been so far.

Art is not ours to judge—
we are judged by art.
We are split open wide,
we are unmasked,
we are unexpectedly delighted
by the lovely dissection
of a profound thought
recorded on the page of
someone's notebook.

Notebook

What is it they see on a page?
Beauty? Eloquence?
Prolific intelligence?

All these notebooks,
ragged and worn around the edges,
from the days she pulled them out
and scrawled her frustration,
cradled her love,
circled her way into hope.
They are battered,
perhaps a bit brittle
from the opening,
from the closing.
But within them sits
her world.

She did not start them
so that others could know her
but so that she could know herself.
And her very essence is there,
held within the pages, speaking
to all who dare open them.

Some of her pages are falling apart.
Some of them are seaming back together.
She has been lovingly handled
by some who read her pages
and felt the making of their own hearts.
She has been hatefully read by others,
combed for all the mistakes,
all the words left out,
all the erroneous beliefs and choices
triumphantly pointed out
by those who would try
to unmake her.
Those who never could.

She has sat on shelves,
she has lounged on beds, tables, chairs,
she has been shoved in a satchel, hidden away.
She has lived in plain view
and in the artfully veiled
places.

Her pages number the years—
the one where a man up and left,
the one where a beloved ringed her
in silver and promised forever,

the one where children
begged for attention at every turn.
She has seen it all.
She has told the stories,
she has watched her pages turn
with delight at times,
with sorrow, too.

Say what you will
about this notebook,
but she is not afraid of life.
She has lived.
She has contemplated.
She has witnessed
all there is to bear,
and though ragged
and worn around the edges,
her pages still turn.
Her volumes still speak.
Her covers still hold.

Gift

No one could ever doubt
the power of a word
to break a heart and
mend it whole again.
A spoken word can save a life;
so, too, can written words
cleanse a soul.
But when a pen becomes still
in a writer's hands,
when rhythm falls asleep,
a breath will catch
a thousand jagged moments,
dying until a word
shakes free again.

Life, then, moves
between the words,
indebted to imagination's
gift.

The Book

crack it open
there are worlds within pages

adventures and mysteries
and the essence of life
contained in history, science, story

teaching, widening memory,
affirming identity, all gathered
in a single spine
in a small collection of paper

so when a day has given
all it can give and there is nothing
left to do or see or glean or learn or try,
there is still
the book.

Write

What's the point?
I can't get the words
flowing today.
Maybe it's because
I put so much pressure
on myself.
Write this, write that,
every day it's another story
and before I know it,
everything's all jumbled up
in my mind, all ideas
I can't seem to extract
from my subconscious.
So I try to read,
but that voice comes sliding in—
they're so much better,
you'll never be this good,
you should give up,
and I think, *Yeah,*
I should give up,
because what's the point?

But instead I

take my pen in hand
and write.

I Write

I write so I can
discover what is
mysterious about the world
to me.

I write so I can
bring my clouded thoughts
into a clarity of purpose
and mind.

I write so I can
figure out the past
and turn it into something
more beautiful.

I write so I can
think and feel and
understand what is
not understandable
to me.

I write to preserve
a moment in time,

snap a picture
with words.

I write to
meander through
the maze of
my mind.

I write to gather
my dreams close
and give them
wings.

I write to fight off
depression, anxiety,
anger, fear,
hopelessness,
suicide,
death.

I write to
find peace,
love,
hope.

I write
to discover
who I am,
to love myself.

I write to uncover
memories, sorrows,
hurts, joys, dreams,
plans, feelings.

I write to forgive the people
who have hurt me, embarrassed me,
discounted me, protected me, stripped me,
celebrated me, misunderstood me,
hated me, loved me.

I write to embrace
every experience as a shaping,
a rounding off of my hard edges,
a softening of the points.

I write to
dust off the
diamond of
truth.

I write to breathe,
to grip order
in chaos,
to love.

I write to
change the world
and me with it.

Poem

He beams before a glowing cake,
a little embarrassed that
we're all looking at him,
singing him a song while he wears
that silly stretched out smile
and the light dances on his face
and flickers in his eyes.
Click.

They stand in line
against the fence,
waiting for the shout
that will tell them to move,
pick up their balls,
in every color of the rainbow,
and begin lobbing them at us.
Click.

Jagged pieces of wrapping
strewn about the living room,
which was perfectly clean
only hours before.
Now it's covered

in a celebration
of him.
Click.

They press into corners, opening their books,
folding them open and then closed,
looking for the next one,
all those discarded volumes
waiting on the floor,
a voice calling through it all
in the cadence of story.
Click.

All of it I gather,
to be used, later,
in a poem.

What I Love About Writing

What I love about writing
is that we must imagine
a thousand realities
and insert ourselves
into the lives of others.
We must become them—
feel their disappointment, their pain,
their worry, the weight of their humanity.
We must understand and experience,
rather than turn a blind eye.
We must live a thousand lives
and live them all well.
We must become the voice
of our people.

What I love
about writing
is its greatness.

Quiz

You write because…
a. You want to be famous
b. You want to be great
c. You want to be known
d. You want to get out of bed

You write fiction because…
a. You want to be famous
b. You want to be great
c. You want to be known
d. You want to rewrite your childhood

You write essays because…
a. You want to be famous
b. You want to be great
c. You want to be known
d. You want to face your memories

You write poetry because…
a. You want to be famous
b. You want to be great
c. You want to be known
d. You want to make sense of this chaotic world

An Ode to the Book

It smells musty,
like a thousand fingers
have passed these pages.

It shifts when I crack it,
falling open in the exact place
it needs in order to feel
most comfortable in my hands.
The words flash out at me,
begging for my attention,
and as I read, a story world
builds around me, replacing
the real-life scene in which
a lover sits on the side of a bed,
one leg touching mine,
watching a movie.
I am no longer here,
no longer the reader holding
an old book with a faded red cover.
I am no longer separate from
this treasure I hold. I am inside it.

Page after page,

I feel, smell, see, hear, taste,
every sense alive with expectation.
I smell the years in the paper,
I feel significance in
its rough leather cover,
I hear the whisper of progress,
I taste humanity on my finger
when I wet it to unstick a page
on which there is a smear of chocolate.

This book has pencil marks,
notes jotted in its margins,
the handwriting of someone
who found it necessary
to mark a passage for later.
I read the notes, imagine
the person who scrawled them
in such beautiful script,
wonder what this book
might have meant
to him or her.

Friends are reading
on electronic devices now.
You take one lightweight gadget,

loaded with ten or more books, they tell me,
eyeing my backpack filled to the brim
with the choice I couldn't make today.
But it's not the same.
They know this, too.

My back may ache
from carrying around
these volumes bound in leather,
stitched with thread and glue,
but the turning of pages,
this sensory engagement
that feels sacred and connective,
cannot be replaced.

A book is a treasure,
passed down through the ages,
collecting stories of its own.

Like a Bookshelf

It's Nineteen Eighty Four.
The Stranger is Beloved
but Death Comes for the Archbishop
and The Talented Mr. Ripley
stands on The Road,
staring at The Magic Mountain,
where The Golden Bowl meets
The Moonstone and raises
Demons from their Pale Fire.
They stalk Little Women,
aggravate Pride and Prejudice,
dry out First Love like A Raisin in the Sun.
Wives and Daughters,
Sons and Lovers,
Women in Love
become The Beautiful and the Damned.
The House of Mirth becomes
the Bleak House, where
Things Fall Apart and unity
is more like War and Peace,
by turns a Catch 22 and The Color Purple,
Les Miserables for Great Expectations,
where one no longer knows

The Name of the Rose or
what it means to
Love in the Time of Cholera.
Not even Doctor Zhivago can
set this Animal Farm to rights.

Speak, Memory.
Show Dead Souls
The Sound and the Fury,
what it means to return
To The Lighthouse.

This is The Portrait of a Lady:
Mrs. Dalloway, carried away on
The Wings of the Dove,
for One Hundred Years of Solitude.

Measure

What is the measure
between a sunrise and a sunset?
They're roughly the same,
displaying similar colors,
if a bit bolder in one than the other.
Pale yellow, golden orange,
pink and purple, depending
on which we view.
But the measure is all different,
some days easy to love,
others feeling like love
is the most difficult of
all things.

And what does that glow
hold in its beauty?
Is it hope? Dreams?

A day's end?
A brand new
beginning?

Perhaps it is all of these.

Perhaps, too, it is not the beauty
or the magnificence or even
the fading or brightening of color
that matters nearly as much as
what happens in the realms of blue.

For we are born
and we die and
what lives in between
is what goes on and on
forever.

Silences

What about the silences?

It was an odd question,
what about the silences,
and I wasn't entirely sure
how to answer.

The silences are long.
The silences are still.
The silences are…
silent.

Yes, but are they
comfortable? she said,
and this time I understood—
because I'd been in
uncomfortable silences before,
and they were awkward, uneasy,
frightening at times.

No, I said,
the silences are
lovely pockets of time

when I can hear myself think
and he can hear himself not think
and we are separate yet connected.

Then you know, she said.
Silences tell you
everything about
a relationship.
So measure them
well.

A Family Recipe

¼ cup of sugar
He gives me a kiss
square on the nose
and leaves his slobber
for later.

¼ cup of butter
He slides past the door
like it's nothing.
I didn't lock
the deadbolt
fast enough.

2 eggs
They spin and fly
on the trampoline,
cracking each other's heads
and laughing about it.
Guess they can be
put back together, then.

½ tsp vanilla
He flavors everything

with Encouragement,
Patience, and Hope.

1 cup flour
He's the baseline,
the leader of the pack,
the bulk of
creative output.

¼ tsp baking soda, ¼ tsp salt
And without him,
it would all
fall flat.

The Happiness of Life

He clomps down the stairs,
taking two or three at a time.
I'm in the kitchen,
listening to something,
dishing oatmeal into bowls
like I always do on
Wednesday mornings.
The first thing he does
is pull me away from the
bamboo spoon waiting to be filled,
wrap me in his arms, and
kiss me long and deep
in a way that my lips
will remember long
after he leaves for work.

Their sounds fill the kitchen,
bowls to be put away,
lunches to be made,
folders to be signed and packed up,
shoes to be located,
last-minute homework tended to,
but in the madness of it all,

one of them places a hand on my arm,
brings my face down to his,
kisses me on the cheek,
says, "Thank you for
fixing us breakfast
every morning."

I watch them in the backyard
while I scribble a few things
in a notebook, frantically trying
to capture what will soon slip away,
and when I'm finished I look up,
catch his eye.
He smiles largely enough
to encapsulate me in a
warm bubble of joy
so intense we can
hardly contain it.

This is what
the happiness of life is:
minute fractions of time
that seem tiny when compared to
the whole of a life
but stamp into memory

a kiss, a word,
a smile that lives for
all eternity.

Forever

1 + 1 + love + ring + vows + hard work =
Forever

What We Do

On our street
someone dumped a load
of what looks like crystals
tinged with rust
and my sons stick
their hands in it,
drawing patterns, painting,
making art out of chemical,
and though it brings them joy,
it brings me sadness,
because this is the world
we live in, where people
don't care how they destroy
the earth's beauty,
where it's just another
day in the life.
I call to my sons,
make them go scrub their hands,
remind them that they've been told
not to play with whatever's been dumped,
and as they elbow past me, I wonder:
How much of this beauty
will be left for them?

What we do to the earth
is what we do
to ourselves.

Rain

The drops smear
a world on my window,
and I cannot help but
follow them outside,
to the street, to the grass,
to the dry ground
that welcomes them.
I cannot help but
lie down and wait for their
gentle kiss, their cold breath,
their melody to whisper its washing.
The very world they contain
splashes over me, and I know
that I contain this world, too.
I let them beat, let them drop,
let them sting and staunch and stain.

I let them stay.

The Natural World

If one wanted to know
what it means to be patient,
one would only have to
observe the way trees grow,
so slowly you don't even notice,
you simply wake up one day
to see green leaves with
brown felt on their bottoms
and white flowers opening
into a gray sky, hanging
over your head.
Ten years it took this tree
to become a resting place that
infuses the yard with the
smell of magnolia.
Ten years it did not hurry
but merely stretched into majesty.

If one wanted to know
what it means to be persistent,
one would only have to take
a good, long look at the grass,
trod on every day by little feet

walking home from school,

playing soccer,

picking flowers.

It yellows at the edges,

heat turning it brittle.

Occasionally it is uprooted by

curious hands searching for pill bugs.

And yet year after year,

season after season

it remains.

It finds a way to

continue existing,

enduring,

growing.

And so, on the days

I want to fold up and give in,

I pull open my back door

and fix my eyes upon the trees,

rest my feet upon the grass,

remember the patience and persistence

of the natural world

that is mine in

equal measure.

A Scientific Questionnaire

i

Why do we do what we do?
How can we act differently?
What keeps us from doing the unthinkable?
Can we replicate more of it?

ii

What causes anger?
What does hatred have to teach us?
What have we done with our expectations for being human?

iii

What does our digital world do to our emotional stability?
What can we do to practice empathy?

iv

Who are you?
Who am I?
What links us together?

v

What is the relationship between what I want and what you want?

How do we both get what we want?

vi

How do we find our way in a world of terror?
How do you find courage to be a parent?
How do you parent without damaging your children?
What would cause a mother to strike her child?
How do you teach your children about love, mercy, justice, empathy, tolerance, truth, hope, wonder, dreams, intelligence, relationships?

vii

How do we improve ourselves?
How do we improve our society?
How can we expect more?
How can we expect less?
What is tolerance?
How do you make concessions without losing yourself?

viii

What is the shape of this world?
How could we shape it differently?
What causes a person to pick up a gun and shoot a Russian ambassador because of a political preference?
How might we step in the path of that bullet and stop it

from meeting its intended mark?
Would we find it imperative?

ix

What kind of love is this?

x

How do we create a better society, a new knowledge, without asking a whole world of new questions?

The Known World

What is the known world?
Is mine the same as yours?
Do we see colors
exactly like another,
red on fire in the setting sun,
green that lifts a heart toward spring,
violet that calms with a flicker?
Do we look upon
the same sky and clouds,
shaped like a rabbit eating
a fluffy white carrot?
Or is it all some
grand illusion that our brains
put on for show?

What is the known world?
Is the person sitting next to me
really there, or does he
shimmer at the edges,
gone in the blink of an eye?
This house we share,
the children clattering through halls,
the flowers out back,

do they exist, or are they
intricate creations of my imagination?

What is the known world?
Is it a thing we can touch
and see and taste,
or does it all live in the mind,
the control center of our reality?
Am I here at all?

What is the known world?

Thunderstorms

When I was a kid,
I had a love-hate relationship
with thunderstorms.
I hated them, because
they were scary,
rumbling, thundering,
tearing across the flatland
with a roar that shook
the foundation of our home.
They always seemed much more
dangerous than they really were.
I didn't understand their power.
I didn't understand their majesty.

On the nights it stormed,
my mother would let us stay up late,
pull out our sleeping bags,
pile in the living room,
all of us together,
the windows flashing and rattling.
So I loved thunderstorms, too,
because what they meant
at the heart of them was

family togetherness.
They came to represent
some of my sweetest
childhood memories.
A thunderstorm would break
through the night, and their warmth
would peel away the barrier of
aloneness that plagued my childhood.
Their light would illuminate
the chasm of one missing
and the one who remained,
proving she was a
big enough presence
to fill the gap.

The thunderstorm had nothing
on the four of us huddled
in a living room,
comforted into sleep.

The Fragility of the Earth

We're walking to school together,
and it's clear, even on the
short half-mile walk, that people
don't really care about the earth.

Soda bottles hug curbs.
Candy wrappers flap like flags,
caught between two blades of grass.
An old fast food bag,
with the trash that tells of
almost everything consumed
except for a few fries, crunches
beneath the tires of careless cars.
No one stops to pick any of it up,
put it where it belongs.
Not even me.

My sons stop to hassle a snail,
on its way to who knows here.
They stop to examine a busy ant pile,
waves crawling across the indentation
of a shoe that, from its simple print,
leaves no indication as to whether

this disturbance was accidental or purposeful.
They pause to pick flowers in the field
beside their school, and I am struck, momentarily,
by how beautiful this earth is,
by how solid it appears but
how very fragile it actually is.

I wonder if my children's children
will be able to stop and trace
the shiny path of a snail.
I wonder if my children's children
will bend to observe an anthill come alive.
I wonder if they will have the pleasure
of dancing in a field of flowers,
picking handfuls of purple and white
to thrust at their mother.
I hope they do.
I want to make sure they do.

But then we are back home,
where the madness of life
tornadoes around me,
and I forget about the
fragility of the earth,
in favor of my own fragility.

And I know, then, why people forget
to care about the earth.
Life is much more
urgent.

The Weather

The day I lost my job,
the sun did not hide its face
but scorched my cheeks
in rolling waves of fire,
but the day my boyfriend
asked me to spend forever
by his side, the streets were
glistening with water that
dropped in sheets from the sky.

It poured on my wedding day,
but the day my beloved grandmother died
and the whole world moved on
with a giant hole in it,
not a cloud stood
in the winter sky.
The sun beamed as though
this day were full of joy.
It wasn't.

The night my first son
slid into the world,
the sky held no stars,

only a heavy black sky,
ominous and uneasy,
but the night my daughter died
was a diamond one,
glittery and full.

So, you see, the weather
never quite
gets it right.

Snoring

Nature converses
outside my window,
creaks and groans and
songs of summer,
a thousand insects joining
in a melody that we
cannot understand, only feel.
I listen, unable to name them all—
that low drone of a bullfrog,
the chirping of crickets,
the hum of grasshoppers,
a dog now and then,
from a neighboring house.
It goes on and on and on,
and I listen until
the one beside me
drifts into a sleep that
must be deep and satisfying—
the noise he releases into the night
drowns out the din of all
the others.

A Very Good Life

In the spring you are born,
red and new and shining.
You see the world in a brilliant way—
the golden glow of sunshine,
the green lace of buds
covering the trees,
flowers of every color,
which you'll pick for your mother.
You run through earthy-smelling fields,
pointing out butterflies and
caterpillars clinging to grass,
staring up at the nests that hold
tiny baby birds.
Spring is all wondrous,
all exciting,
all curiously entertaining.

In the summer you laugh
out on the back deck with
friends and family, enjoying
the feel and rhythm of the intimate,
the rope of togetherness.
You dip your toes in the ocean,

take long walks along beaches
and through shadowy woods,
insects humming around your head,
a hand sweating in your own.
You retreat to the shade when
it gets a bit too bright and warm.
Summer is all heat,
all energetic,
all domestically vibrant.

In the fall, the air whispers
of an easier time, a cooling off,
a relaxation period that is not
necessarily better but different.
Children are gone,
and with them demands,
and now it's just the two of you
wrapped in an embrace,
wondering where all the
interruptions and requests
and loud raucous mornings
have gone and how on earth
they disappeared so quickly,
before you knew it, really.
Leaves fall to the ground,

leaving their gilded colors
and their bittersweet truths.
Fall is all love,
all quiet,
all wistfully reminiscent.

In the winter, the world
becomes brittle, limbs bare
and twisting. The skin grows cold,
and the long walks must be abandoned
in favor of shorter ones, to see
the world outside your window.
You spend nights by the fireside,
a book open in your lap.
Visitors come and go,
die off one by one, and you feel
the cold aching in your heart,
the holes of loss and missing.
You wish you could have frozen time,
made it last longer,
but time has a mind of its own.
Winter is all wonder,
all memories,
all cleanly mysterious.

Spring, summer, fall, winter—
they all add up to
a very good life.

The Wind

A wind works against the dark,
stirring up all sorts of debris,
clanking cans, shaking plastic lights,
rattling children's outdoor toys
all through the street.
Whirlwinds scatter
brown, withered leaves
that long ago lost their hold on the trees.
Bushes bend in a breath
that's turned unexpectedly cold.
We watch the front move
across the canyon from our
second floor window.
We watch it knock against
the lovers leaning on a streetlamp,
turn over the welcome mats on doorsteps,
extinguish the lights.

We don't say a word,
both of us wishing
the wind in the
corners of our minds
could turn us inside out, too.

The Leaf

The sky is a perfect blue,
winking at me between the leaves
that remain clinging to the trees.
Wind puffs on the playground,
swirling around a little boy
in a long-sleeved shirt, blue,
too heavy for the warmth of the day.
He is barefoot, holding a carrot
that clanks into a metal container
when he decides he is done with it.
Five others creak and screech
on swings, the wind blowing them back,
their legs pumping them forward.
I wait beneath a tree, watching
from a green picnic bench,
memorizing the sky,
the feel of the wind,
the laughter,
the promise of fall.

Leaves dance in the
middle of the playground.
The sun glimmers off an

orange slide, brass bolts
holding it together.
Rusty chains hang
from the swings.
The colors in this view
are vibrant, brilliant,
a representation of
photographic art.

The barefoot child
gazes up at the sky.
The wind ruffles his white curls.
Leaves wave at him,
and he waves back.
He stares at them for a time,
picks one up and
brings it to his mother.
He is trying to figure out his world,
just as I am trying to figure out mine.
So I hold the leaf,
turn it over,
listen to what it might
say to me.

The Display

I tilt my head to the side.
What is it? I say.
He stands beside me,
looking much the same as me.
I don't really know, he says.
It's a person, sitting on a stool,
wrapped in burlap. Simple
and yet meaningless,
a molded figure.
I might have made it myself.

We stand there a moment longer
and then move on because
there are many more displays
that wait to be seen, observed,
understood as best they can.
But a guard stops us, points back
to the figure behind us.

She made it after World War II, he says.
He draws us back
to the burlap display.
She lived through it.

In a concentration camp.
She was a Jew who had been
thrown away, and she wanted
to make art of what was easily
thrown away. Burlap.

He turns to us and grins.
He is missing a tooth at the
bottom on the left.
He does not say more
but lets the words hang.

We linger, staring at the figure
making beautiful what
might have been thrown away,
making worthy what
did not seem valuable,
and now, in our notice,
it is more than
a figure wrapped in burlap,
because it means something good,
something holy,
something important.
And it is more than art,
because it speaks of truth.

Just like that, a display that one might pass
without a second look becomes
a display that begs one to
sit and contemplate and wonder.

The Birth of Art

I didn't know
that you could take in
so much through the eyes.

I didn't know that you could
find inspiration in a
corn field full of golf balls

we hunted like Easter eggs
or a wooden swing hung
from two rusty iron posts

or a sandy head
tilted in the
position of a question.

I didn't know that a walk
along a gravel path would
write within me a song.

I didn't know that a breeze
tearing through hair could
whisper in me a word.

I didn't know that a man,
beside me in a booth,
splitting a plate of dinner,

laughing about the slower,
less-complicated days,
could kiss me with a poem.

But now I do.

The Popularity Contest

Art isn't what it used to be.

We used to be able to create in obscurity, to hide away in our painting rooms or writing rooms or composing rooms, but now our art has become public, perhaps before we're even ready for it to do so. We share never-ending videos and inside looks at our process and our trade secrets, though I've never been one to hide trade secrets. But sometimes it feels like we can't ever create in private, because to make it as artists in this social world, we have to open up the doors and windows of our creative lives and let people in.

Sometimes I don't want to let people in.

Art has become a popularity contest. It all depends on how many hearts you get on that painting you posted, or how many people visited the site where you shared that excerpt from a work-in-progress, or how well you cropped the musical sample. It matters how many followers click the button, the kinds of comments you accrue ("Beautiful!" "So true!" "I want to hear more!"), the pieces of the whole you cut up and pass out.

Art was never supposed to be a popularity contest. When we make it one, we have lost the very essence of art, that strange capacity to elicit private emotions in the hearts of our audience.

So maybe it's time to start creating in obscurity again, closing our doors, shutting down our video cameras, spending time alone with our art and the mysterious process of creation.

The Point of Art

—What is it?

I don't know.

—You don't know what it is?

I don't know what it is to you.

—But what is it to you?

That's irrelevant.

—But isn't that what makes art—understanding it?

Art isn't necessary to understand.

—Then what's the point?

The point is love.

—That doesn't even make sense.

Art is given meaning by the people who love it.

By the love with which it was created.

By the love it creates within.

—So this piece?

Is art.

The Artist's Tradition

The Internet culture—that's what they call it. It's the increasing population of people who believe that if something is on the Internet it should be free. It is the population of people who unwittingly devalue art by expecting its gift. It is the population of people who sit on their wallets and explore only what is given.

We, the artists, are told by expert marketers to offer ourselves and our art for a price that readers, consumers, will find acceptable—99 cents, say, or, better yet, free, regardless of the months or years spent in the making and perfecting of it.

What is the future of the Internet generation? An entitlement to all art that could mean an end to the artist's tradition.

Through the Lens

Through the lens of a camera
I watch their faces
distorted at the edges
but clear in the middle
where brown and blue
and the slightest hint of green
stare back at me
if they notice
I see them play
I witness them giggle

Through the lens of a camera
the day is magnified
and I find the dimple on his cheek
that summons a second glance
the gap between his bottom teeth
that will likely need
fixing someday
a hole in his white sock

Through the lens of a camera
the earth comes alive—clear
more beautiful perhaps

because the lens of a camera
offers a look at what has
never been seen:
still life seconds snapped
into forever memory

Through the lens of a camera
I am reminded of
the smell of his skin
when he was only hours old
the bittersweet taste of his
growing independence
the sight of his hand
reaching for mine and
actually
remarkably
staying for a while

Through the lens of a camera
my world takes shape
a shadowy kiss
a sun-splashed face
a moment stolen in the wild
framed in time

Through the lens of a camera
I walk back to thanks
to love
to peace

The Song

The song of a bird
raised on the wind
is a melody unlike
any other,
and in the yard,
where they play on a trampoline,
I listen to the beauty
that has nothing to do with
what I can see and
everything to do with
the distant music
of a creature that knows
how to sing of love
and joy and
hope.

Music

They watch
we work
and there is a rhythm to this
writing, designing, planning,
and then, in the middle of it,
their laughter shuttles toward us,
wild and unconfined and contagious,
and we close our computers,
search for their faces,
and get lost in the sound,
all words unnecessary
in the bubbling wonder of
music.

Sing

You think that maybe
you can do it again,
but it's time, and your
throat closes up and you
look at him wide-eyed,
shaking your head,
even though you've done this,
this very thing,
since you were four,
and you've done it
with him for nearly a decade,
and you didn't even
get nervous after a
certain point because
you knew what you
were doing.

You knew what you
were doing.

At least you knew
what you were doing
until a man you

knew and respected
told you that you were
playing in the big leagues now
and you didn't make the cut,
and now every time it's time,
you can't. You're too afraid,
because what if he was right,
what if you're not really as good
as you thought you were,
what if they all see it,
or, rather, hear it, too?

It's time.
You open
your mouth.
And sing.

Who We Are

The soul of us is
music, poetry, words
wrapped in melody
or a silent background

We may see the killing,
the blood running in the streets,
the slanderous shaming,
the nit picking and the
finger-pointing,
we may feel the
desperate longing for a
better day, we may know
that things can't continue on
in this way without breaking
the whole world in two,
and we may feel it all the way
to the marrow of our bones,
shame, fear, anxiety, dislike,
maybe even hate

The whole world
may be falling apart,

but the worst of it
cannot touch our soul,
our music,
our poetry,
our words

It will rise,
more beautiful, more intense,
more marvelous than ever
Because we are still alive,
and this is
who we are

Though We Wandered

We wander,
waiting, wondering, seeking,
gold glitters in the distance
and we take off running its way,
thinking we have found
the whole answer to life,
because it shines and
it sparkles and it will surely
lend its light over all
that comes next

And then we are there,
neck even, right in front of it,
and we see the blemishes,
the scratches, the chips
along the sides, and maybe
it wasn't, in fact, the
whole answer to life, because
the whole answer to life
would be more beautiful,
less rusted,
flawless

So we wander,
waiting, wondering, seeking,
our feet grown more numb
in a frost that does not
reach roots, thank God,
because it's cold and wet
and slimy between the toes

The sun scorches our cheeks,
drawing red like muted blood
in patches across our skin
and there is no relief to this
never-ending wasteland,
where we wander

The only hope
this horizon has
to offer is
an old rock

An old rock
where once had been
a golden masterpiece

Our future bundled up

in a shiny image

If only, if only, if only

We climb the rock
We stand
We look

And there before us is a
view of the land we have crossed
through days and weeks
and in and out of years
and how did we miss
how lovely light could be
when dressed in white

We did not see
But this old rock
This old rock

It is an ancient respite,
a resting place that
lays bare truth:
though we wandered,
we were not lost

Unforgotten Home

I didn't want to stay.
Anyone who became someone
got out of there as
fast as they could,
the wide open cornfields
waving them down the street,
like their own personal
send-off committee.

When I think of home,
I think of trains splitting
the calm of night, followed by
the sounds of wolves
howling in the distance,
followed by a silence so thick
it hurt my ears. You could see
the stars there like nowhere else
on earth, shimmering in a sky
so black I could imagine it was
the open mouth of a cave
full of loneliness.
Mosquitos followed good blood
into rooms and droned in ears

all night, stealing nourishment
during the sleeping hours,
leaving welts that would
last for days.

Mornings tasted like
sweet oranges and the
soft waters of the bay.
Afternoons smelled of wildflowers
and the sweat of hard work.

Life moved at its
own pace there.
I couldn't wait to leave.

And now, when I am
lying in my bed at night,
my husband asleep beside me,
my children dreaming in their beds,
I often think of that
black cavern of starlight,
the howling wild,
the sharp sting of a bite,
the sweet taste of sustenance,
the smell of heat.

Sometimes I even miss it.

But anyone who became someone
got out of there as
fast as they could.

The Unanswerable

Where am I going, you ask?
Well, that's not so simple to say,
because I don't really know.
I just step out into the
great nothingness and hope
I've picked the right way.

People say it's important
to know where you're going
and whether it's the right direction,
but people don't understand
how hard that is for the
directionally challenged.
I was the kid who used to
argue with my mother
on the way to church,
because I knew for a fact
that she was going the wrong way,
and ten minutes later, we pulled up
in front of the church.
I was shocked every time.
How was it that we had headed
in the wrong direction

yet still made it?

Point your steps
down the right path,
choose the right direction,
try to find your own way,
it sounds easy enough when
you're not me, but then again,
who am I, really, and who
do I want to be?
I don't know.
Does that mean
I'll never know?

The roaring and thrumming
from outside shakes inside,
someone doing improvements
on their already-improved house,
installing better wood floors
or spraying on a layer of paint
or repairing the roof tiles.
When it reaches me,
blasting me out of
my contemplation,
my first thought is this:

Hell, what does it matter?
At least I'm alive.

The Distance Between

The moon is full tonight.
He is somewhere in a bar,
shut away inside with his hand
curled around a drink,
probably a Budweiser,
unaware of the moon
glowing outside my window.
This was always
the distance between us—
the romantics said no matter
how many miles away
you might be from one another,
you could always see the same
moon and stars dangling
above your head,
but there is a distance
that cannot be measured in miles.
It is much harder to quantify.

The distance between
A and Z is
twenty-four letters.
The distance between

Texas and Ohio is
two thousand miles.
The distance between
the heart of a father and
the heart of a daughter is
immeasurable,
impassible,
impossible.

I pull my covers
to my chin and
turn away from the moon
that is only mine to see.

The Fibers of a Photograph

The light falls just so,
illuminating her face,
erasing the lines
time marked on skin.
She does not notice
the still frame snapped.
I draw back,
examining the corners,
sun and shadow
crossing at all the right angles,
transforming her into
something other-worldly,
something entirely unknown,
something hushed and sacred
and invincible.
She sees me watching
through the lens,
says, *Don't take*
a picture of me, I don't even—
but I do not listen, of course.
I snap them anyway,
until the light sinks too far
and the shadows creep

from the corners and
her face is no longer distinguishable
against the back of the couch.
I cannot see her now,
but she lives on,
etched into the fibers
of a photograph.

The Run

I used to run
down a dirty path
to a canal that would
irrigate the cornfields
surrounding my mother's
house. It was nothing special—
a road that held the gorges
of harvest tractors, and,
most likely, the fumes of
pesticides that clung
to my lungs.

I ran to be skinny.
I ran to have a better body,
because I had lost myself
among so many alike.
We were girls trying to
adhere to a standard
set by our society.
I did not have the perfect body,
I had one that needed work
to sculpt and shape into
the ideal image.

I plunged myself headlong
into the pursuit, and that's why,
when I was sixteen and
had a spare moment in which
I was not hunched over homework
or practicing my clarinet,
I gravitated toward the
uneven dirt path that cut
between rows of corn my brother
would pick when we needed
a little something more to eat.
I ran to shed the pounds,
and it was only later that
I would learn they were not
simply physical pounds,
they were emotional pounds,
and I ran to shed
every one of them.

On one such run, birds perched
on power lines and hid in the grass.
Corn plants rustled around me,
dried out from a hot summer.
The air was stifling on that
road through sustenance.

I looked ahead at the ending place,
the canal that formed
the halfway point and then
I looked down at my feet.
I took those first springing steps,
birds erupting all around me
like a wave of black feathers.
Their wings set my tempo,
their squawks set my song,
their scare, the way they turned a mind
toward Alfred Hitchcock's "The Birds"
set my feet flying faster than
they'd ever run before.
A couple of them flew
alongside me for a time
but dropped away in silence,
much like the memory
of the one who had been absent
for the last five years.

And as I felt the weights
begin to drop around me,
a burning belted into my chest,
and my footsteps rang out my awakening.
I am strong, they said.

I am beautiful.
I am loved.
I am enough.

I found myself on the
grooved dirt road that
stretched between my mother's home
and a field where corn plants
turned their ears toward
my newfound freedom,
huffing in and out of
my chest.

The Windows

The brambles have grown up
over the windows of
my childhood home
They are boarded up
with new wood, smelling
of pine and strength and mystery,
and the arms of the vines
that reach across them
dry out, wither,
die

It appears that this is for the best
Remove the brambles and the
boarded up windows wrench free,
so the hand waiting behind them
can nudge, push, fling them wide open
and what is inside meets
what is outside without
a single thought,
in its frenzied movement,
for hiding

Perhaps, when we let the brambles die,

when we push the windows open,
when the inside meets the outside,
we choose what to keep,
what to discard,
what, essentially, to overlook,
and we begin to recognize
all the sunlight creeping into
the memories of our childhood home,
how beautiful it could be,
how warm, how full of hope
and laughter and love

Perhaps it is meeting
the shadows from
inside those windows
and looking them
full in the face
that saves us
Or perhaps it is
the windows themselves,
looking glasses into
who we were and are,
the shape we have taken since,
that saves us
Perhaps it is both

The windows that were boarded shut
stand, now, nailed open,
redeemed

Where We've Been

We don't like to think about
where we've been,
because it's painful
(the dad who straddled a motorcycle and drove away)
and shameful
(the phone call recorded on a machine, spilling that secret)
and ugly
(the rationing of food to fill a belly or not)

We don't like to talk about
where we've been,
because we've come so far
(first generation college graduate, right here—just crown me successful)
and we're afraid of its hold
(friend number two just stepped right back into her mother's life—I was sure she'd made it)
and we don't want anyone
to see the past display
like a freak show advertisement
(blood, sex, whiskey, anxiety, depression, imagine what you will)
because we're not a

freak show anymore;
our life today is the
closest to normal
it'll ever get

We don't like to admit
where we've been
(at the bottom of nothing),
so we surgically remove
that giant piece of the past
(I only had two pairs of pants when I was in the sixth grade)
and alter our present
(my sons have enough clothes to go a week without wearing
the same thing)
because no one can ever
guess or see or know

But something presses
at the edges,
blurring our focus,
and when we step
close enough to examine it,
we'll see that it's the past,
waving its tangled yarns,
inviting us to remember

and if we can let
our guards down for
one second and
let it speak, we'll see:
it's only in examining
where we've been
that we can clearly see
where it we're headed

Memory

I miss her laugh the most,
the way it would shake itself
out into nothingness,
like all the air had gone
and she could find no more,
but it was a happy place to be.
Sometimes she would get so tickled
my uncle had to slam his hand
against her back to get her
breathing again, but that
made her laugh all the more.

I miss those late nights
I'd spend reading in my room,
during the few summers
I lived with her.
I would make my way
into the bathroom for my
nightly routine of washing a face
and brushing my teeth,
and the dining room light
would still be blazing,
and there she'd sit at the table

in purple slippers with a
crossword puzzle open
in front of her. She'd be
chewing on the end of a pencil,
oblivious to the stacks of papers
shoved in corners. She'd have a
bag of potato chips or Riesen caramels
open and ready at her elbow.

I miss her purple lipstick
that always left traces on her teeth
and the way I would watch her
leave for work at the school
down the road while I
got ready for my own job across town.
She'd always remind me
to lock the door on my way out
and be sure to unplug
the curling iron.
I didn't use a curling iron,
but I never told her that.

I miss seeing her slumped
on the couch in the middle
of the 10 o'clock news, which she

insisted on watching every night,
and I miss the feel of her hand
on mine whenever she was near me.
I miss her curly black-white hair,
and I miss those eyes that never
seemed to miss a thing and the
handwriting in all caps and the
old Agatha Christie volumes
that sat on her shelves,
battered from excessive re-reading.

I miss the way she might have
looked at my sons and the
conversations we might have had
and how tickled she
might have been upon
reading the humor pieces
I carefully crafted with
her in mind.

She did not live a
remarkably extraordinary life,
just one that was remarkably ordinary.
But in my memory,
she is a giant.

My Greatest Endeavor

In grade school, early on, my classmates never
talked of fighting parents. They were too clever.

Before the divorce, my greatest endeavor
was thinking I'd be them. I was so clever.

I didn't talk about loud fights; however,
closed doors don't mute them. They thought they were
clever.

My world tried to spin and fragment and sever
But I could ignore it. I was so clever.

Before the divorce, my greatest endeavor
was wearing my fine mask. I was too clever.

The heated words pushed some invisible lever
so man no longer loved woman. They're clever.

Tension pulled tight and then jagged and never
let a kid catch a break. It was too clever.

Before the divorce, my greatest endeavor

was walking through night fog; I was so clever.

The kids at school asked me questions; whenever
they wondered where Dad was, they weren't so clever.

I didn't know how to answer—wherever
my dad went was mystery. We weren't clever.

And since no one told us anything, ever,
we just had to guess and trust they were clever.

Before the divorce my greatest endeavor
was believing in words. I was so clever.

One day I decided to ask whomever
might know the whole truth—yes, I was so clever.

Turns out, I didn't want to know—whatever
they'd made up was better. I was so clever.

Just a kid who thought they would love forever—
an impossible wish. I was so clever.

Before the divorce my greatest endeavor
was hoping he'd come back. He was too clever.

The Towns of My Life

1
The first town
was quiet enough
to be a ghost town,
neighbors hardly alive
it seemed. My mother
would pull us along the road
to the local post office,
like we had stepped back in time.
We had to cross a highway
to pick up our mail,
and maybe, if we were lucky,
a handful of Bubble Yubble
for 10 cents apiece at the
local gas station. The buildings
were all crammed in along
Highway 111, nestled up close
to the train tracks we'd walk on
when Mama and Daddy
weren't looking.
We lived across the street
from the red-roofed
elementary school with a

metal slide that burned
our backsides in the summer.
If we were really good,
Mama would send us
across the street to the
school playground with a
piece of wax paper, which would
not only lessen the burn
but would also
send us flying down
the impossible heights
at impossible speeds.

That town never really
came alive.
So we left it.

2
The second town
wasn't really a town
so much as it was a road.
Our house was made of stone,
built on a cement floor.
I could tell the difference,
because the floor didn't

bend when I stepped on it.
It was the town where
Mama once picked up
Daddy's shotgun, shoved out
the screen door, and blew to bits
the rattlesnake camped out
on our porch, mesmerizing
our favorite kitten, while we
shouted in the background,
our faces pressed to the screen
that checkered our view
of the whole thing. Guts flew
back onto the door, and we
screamed at the violence of it.
Mama sprayed it down with a hose.
That town had fields painted with
Indian paintbrushes in the spring
and houses too far apart
to yell at neighbors and
cows and coyotes and
another step back into time,
where we were warned away
from water wells,
where Internet didn't exist,
where clouds could dip

into twisters and then
shoot back into the sky.

We were too lonely
in that town.
So we left it.

3
The third town
was freezing cold,
with houses practically
stacked on top of each other,
neighbors who bundled up
so tightly you could never tell
who they were exactly,
but you waved anyway.
They never waved back,
because it wasn't the northern way,
before skidding off down the road.
That town had a school eight blocks
away that we'd walk to every morning,
free skateboarding along
all the sidewalks and stairs,
and a bit of fear built
around the edges.

We were too southern
for that town.
So we left it.

4
The fourth town
was crammed with cars
and stores and houses
everywhere the eye could see.
Trees peeked around
all the corners, but it was
mostly gray and wet enough
in the air to feel like you were
walking under an ocean,
the pressure squeezing
the air from your lungs
while you treaded water
desperately but never
quite broke free.
Or maybe it was only
the circumstances that gave me
that sense of one drizzly day
stretching into an entire year
of drizzly days.

That town had a school
of eight hundred students,
a restaurant where we spent
our straight A coupons
every week, a newspaper
where I'd come back to work
right out of college.

That town was
too loud.
So we left it.

5
The fifth town
was built around a college,
bright green and beautiful.
It had a river where
beautiful people would swim
and sunbathe and play
sand volleyball. It had a
pizza place that sold food cheap
and baseball fields where
a girl could fall in love and
bright lights and glitter
at its top, but a

dull hole in the middle,
when you dug deeper.
That town had long, leisurely runs
and a man-boy scaling a balcony
to save a girl and late late nights
at a newspaper, trying to make
everything perfect so she could
also and more importantly
make herself perfect.

That town was
too immature.
So we left it.

6

The sixth town
was large and sprawling
and yet small and tight.
People smiled at one another
and waved like old friends,
even if they'd never met.
There were shining hotels
that reached for the sky and a
newspaper that laced fact
with memories and the place

where independence was granted
the few men left standing.
There were fountains to be
run through, wooden castles
to be explored, a moon
you could see even with all the
city lights blinking in the distance.
That town had a school
right down the road and
some easily accessible shops and
a library that held what seemed like
every volume of every story
in the world.

That town was
just right.
And so we remained.

That House

We went to see the railroad tracks where my brother and sister and I used to slide down piles of coal and turn our behinds black and then lie to our mother about what we'd been doing (she always knew). We walked the tracks where my cousins and I used to climb on trains and hurtle from one car to another and pretend we were boxcar children. We walked the road past that house.

That house.

That house with the creepy staircase that closed in on its victims, where I could imagine a hand exploding out to grab me every time I needed to go upstairs and take a bath. That house with the long, dark hallway to the unfinished half-bathroom and the back door that never seemed to stay closed all the way, especially on the darkest, stormiest nights. That house where I burned three fingers of my right hand on the lid of a kettle a week before my third-grade standardized test so I had to worry myself through filling in all the bubbles with my left hand.

That house doesn't look so large and scary anymore, and, in a way, I feel like some of the magic has been lifted off, now that I've seen it as an adult.

But then I walked up to the front stoop and stood looking at the familiar door, and a fear gripped me and held me so tightly I could do nothing but flee, to the delighted laughter of my children.

The Wizened Heart

I was only three when
I first knew what it felt like
to have a broken heart.

That was the day
he left the first time,
and I had to go to bed
without a goodnight kiss.

The breaks would come swiftly
after that, from every side—
a death, a death of sorts,
a disappointment, which is like a death.
A word, a look, an unspoken expectation.

I learned that the world
was not to be counted on
for offering kindness,
happiness, goodness,
but that it could often become
ruthless in the worst ways.

My heart did not

become wise until
it had lived through
many more breakings—
a best friend betraying,
a missed opportunity,
a baby lost.

True wisdom
cannot be attained
until
we are
pulled apart
at the seams and
put back
together.

Grandad'n, the Mysterious

i

I remember him as a man who did not speak without some encouragement. He had a great many stories to tell, but it wasn't often that he would sit and tell them, so that meant when he did—the times he stretched out in his chartreuse easy chair rocking every so often with the balls of his large socked feet, the whole room would grow silent, waiting to hear what Grandad'n had to say.

Sitting at his feet, I learned that there was a writer in the family—a newspaper writer, and because I always carried a notebook with me, even as a child, he observed that I would be one, too. I believed him.

ii

He worked out in a garden because he loved the feel of dirt on his skin. He would spend hours at it, even while the rest of his family gathered inside his kitchen and waited on Nana's homemade ice cream. He didn't like crowds, and the garden gave him the wide open space he needed to breathe and think and make sense of his world. I never thought of it as odd, but there are older ones in my family who would call him aloof, unloving, even, a hard man to know. I could understand his need for solitude. I sat on the cement steps of his mobile home and wrote my stories while watching him weed.

iii

I didn't understand why Nana and Grandad'n had separate rooms. At family gatherings, he would sometimes take his meals to his room, as though he preferred the silence of aloneness. He could hear the muffled noise of us behind the closed door, and maybe that was enough for him. He would wander back out eventually. But the thing that always made me wonder was that Nana and Grandad'n had rooms on opposite sides of their house. All the married people I knew slept in the same room, and it was great big mystery to me all my growing up years.

When I was grown, my mother told me that Granddad'n had hit Nana when they were younger. He had fits of anger, suffered from his service in World War II. *Why did she never leave?* I asked, because it was the thing to do in a situation like that. *She loved him*, my mother said, and I found this even more difficult to comprehend. If she loved him so much, why have a separate room? And if she felt safer in her own room, rather than sharing a dark one with him, why stay at all?

iv

I only knew him as a good, kind man.

When I was eight or nine, my great-grandfather had a massive heart attack and died. It was unexpected. He died in his garden, just like he said he wanted to do. But that did not make it any easier for the ones left behind. The wax figure I saw in the casket, the first of its kind that I had ever seen, did not look like him at all. He was never so put together. He wore a suit, which I had never seen him wear. He had only ever worn denim overalls with a white shirt underneath them, as far as my memory could recall. It bothered me immensely to see him in that suit.

A preacher said some words. I watched them lower him into the ground, while I wondered what happened next. Where had he gone? Had he disappeared? Was he now gone forever?

My great-grandmother took me home that night. I slept in her bed to keep her company. I did not even look at his room. I could not stomach it. He visited me that night, though. He told me he was in a better place, that I could go on and live my life, love, be a writer. And then his ghostly form faded away.

In the morning, I did not know for sure whether it had been a dream or some spectral visitation, but I went ahead and lived my life. I went ahead and loved.

I went ahead and became a writer.

The Holes in Memory

There are holes in my memory,
as though someone has sifted through
strings of thought,
patterns of years,
folding away the unnecessary.
I remember nearly everything significant
about my third year—
my near-drowning at a beach,
welcoming a new sister,
muddying a brand new shirt
on the same day I got it,
my father kicking a leg
over the back of a bike
and peeling down the road.

But my tenth year
closed a curtain over memory,
and the scenes come only
in strobe light flashes,
as if, perhaps, they do not
really belong to me,
as if, perhaps, they did not
happen at all.

There are holes in the
linear shape of my life,
where I subconsciously circumvent
certain painful pieces and
extract them from the
story of my past.
But every now and again,
I fall into one of the black holes
and remember why
I forgot it in the first place.

We forget not because we will
but because we must.

A Poor Hand

One might say that I
started out with
all the wrong cards.
Poor parents.
Absent dad.
Little to do in the world
but become the very picture
of my parents before me.
How does one break free
of the cards one has
been dealt?

In sixth grade, my English teacher
told me I had a talent for
dreaming up stories.
In seventh grade, my English teacher
drilled me on proper grammar
and punctuation and spelling,
said I had a gift.
In eighth grade, my English teacher
told me she wanted me to do
some extra writing work,
to develop my emerging skill.

In ninth grade, my English teacher
took my essay on Dickens and
read it to the class while I hid out
in the bathroom, mortified.
He tacked it to the board
as an example of a good critical essay.
In tenth grade, my English teacher
gave me a list of books
I'd need to read
to become a better writer,
said it was optional,
no grade attached.
I read them all.
In eleventh grade, my school counselor
gave me a college application
and said, *No pressure.*
It requires an essay.
I wrote eight hundred words
that night, used the story
of my parents' divorce
to prove that all bad deals
could be turned
into good ones.

The trick to life, you see,

is playing a
poor hand well.

In Praise of Libraries

When I was a little girl,
my mother would take me
to the Jackson County
library every week.
We lived in a tiny town,
with little else to do.

These days were my favorites.
I'd run my hand along
the old book spines,
taking my time choosing
the ones that I would
carry home with me,
the ones that would
carry me away for hours.
I would gather as many
as I could manage
in my spindly arms,
and my mother, knowing that
I would read them all in
the course of a week,
would check out every one of them
and then leave me

to my words.

The library was a place
where the world expanded,
where I learned that it was possible
to be more than just
a poor girl from a poor family
who would never amount
to anything spectacular or significant.
The library brought every possibility
to my fingertips and said
it could happen for me.
The library gave me knowledge
and perspective and a way forward
through every circumstance
that found me.

And so the library
was essential to becoming,
to understanding,
to enduring.

Life As I Knew It

We sat down
for dinner that night.
I have no recollection
what waited in front of us
at the table; the mind
has a way of clearing away
the extraneous details.
I remember my mother
sitting across from us
staring at her hands.
*Your dad and I are
getting divorced*, she said.
Why? we said.
We wanted to make it
hard on her, anger
turning us mean in all the
places that matter.
She had remained for so long—
what made this time different?
Why would she leave him now?

He has another family, she said.
A daughter. A son.

I had known something
was wrong for a long time,
but I had never imagined this.
Another family?
How had it happened?
What had we done wrong?
What was so repellant about us,
the family already made?
I watched my mother's face.
She was strong, resolute.
Traces of anger flashed
intermittently in her eyes.
She had forgiven a whole
lifetime of offenses,
but this could not be forgiven.
It could not be repaired.

We could not be
repaired.

My brother shot out the door,
and me after him.
He headed straight toward
the familiar canal road,

while I stood in the middle
of the street, staring at the sky
that made me feel small and
unnoticed and forgotten.
I had never known
the ache of true sorrow
until that moment.

I was eleven years old
when life as I knew it
ended over dinner.

Legends

Childhood stories
are the stuff
of legends.

There was the time
we saw a ghost standing
on the top of a trash receptacle
while camping for the summer.
She was large and built. Strong.
She carried a baby and a
menacing expression on her
pale, transparent face.
We did not have the courage
to stick around, just turned
and ran as fast as we could,
away from the spectral woman
who would visit our
nightmares that evening.
We told our parents about her,
but of course they didn't believe us.

We saw her again that week,
deep in the woods, tucked inside

an old walled-in, overgrown cemetery
bound by white stones that had
blackened in the crevices
over the years.
No one was supposed to
set foot in that cemetery.
There was a sign forbidding it,
provided someone even *wanted*
to walk among the dead,
which I simply could not fathom.
But my cousin hopped the wall
and stepped on the burial stones,
calling out to us the names that
marked graves as he passed them.
He disappeared in the tall grass
for a moment. She did not show up
until he'd hopped the wall
back to our side and we all
turned for one last look
at remnants of people
we had never known,
and there she stood,
watching us, or watching
something from her past.

The memory of this woman
frames my childhood in gothicity,
turning life into both
a dream and a fear—
one offering all I have
to gain and the other
showing me all I have
to lose.

The Dance

I think I know what I want.
I make my plan to get it,
and, in some way or another,
my plans go up in smoke
and something else comes
hurtling my way.
And at first it doesn't
look like much, but once
my eyes adjust I can see
that what has come my way,
as if by accident,
is better than what
I pursued at first.
Had I known,
it would have been
exactly what I wanted.

And the dance
begins
again.

In Another Life

In another life
    I might have been one of them, investigating the dark secrets of a city.

In another life
    I might have settled down with someone else or chosen to live alone.

In another life
    I might not have lived in a house so destroyed by children.

In another life
    I might have been wealthy, unworried about money.

In another life
    I might not have lain next to you to watch that movie tonight.

In another life
    I might not feel so tired all the time.

In another life

I might have been able to keep a plant alive for more than six months.

In another life
> I might be able to spend a whole year without the pleasure of sugar.

In another life
> I might have written a bestseller.

In another life
> I might not have picked up a pen at all.

In another life
> I might have followed that path all the way to Hollywood.

In another life
> I might have applied makeup for all the stars.

In another life
> I might have been able to leave my family for another state.

In another life

  I might have given her a little more time before she died.

In another life
  I might have chosen to stick with music.

In another life
  I might not have said yes.

In another life
  I might have worn heels.

In another life
  I might have looked in the mirror and seen someone beautiful looking back.

In another life
  I might have been a girl with a dad who did not leave me.

In another life
  I might have chosen to robe myself in bitterness, rather than forgiveness.

In another life

I might have died.

Silence

In the early mornings,
when their daddy
packs them up for the
walk to school, it means
a moment to breathe,
to walk through the halls
of a home that shakes
with laughter and loud voices
and joyous screeching,
to stretch in the warmth of
a moment to myself.

In midmorning,
it means nothing good,
since they're silent when they
don't want to be caught
bluing their hand with a permanent marker
or cutting curious holes in their shirt
or taking some leftover paint to a wall
or tearing up all my notecards
into tiny little irretrievable pieces.

In midafternoon,

it means one stretched
on the floor, feet in the air;
one on his side hugging a couch;
and one bouncing a knee in the armchair,
all of them with a book
in front of their faces.

In the late afternoon,
it means boys crouched
over their devices for a
bit of technology time,
a brief stretch of peace
before they're back to
rifling through the refrigerator
or slamming the door
on their way outside or
walking upstairs to listen
to an audiobook.

In the evenings,
it means the silent treatment,
because they want to
stay up all night.

In the late evenings,

it means scratching out
a few lines in a notebook
and ending a day's work
with a few tired remains.

Ghosts and Monsters

He wants it all
I can see it in his eyes
but mostly I can hear it
in his voice
I understand
I do
I miss the music too
but sometimes a ship sails
and no matter how hard and fast
you run after it
you can never catch it
because it was never
your ship to begin with
He brings it up again
to pick a fight even though
he says he didn't start the conversation
with a fight on his mind
but logic says this is the way
the last twelve conversations
have gone about this particular topic
He wants to do music again
he misses it
he feels like

he can't do it without me
because I'll get bitter
and I listen to the
same old song and think why can't
he be like my brother-in-law
who puts art dreams on hold
for his provision responsibility
why can't this be a dream that
doesn't leave me at home all the time
with six kids and few resources
why can't he just give it up
I fume in my quiet way
afraid to speak up because of
the fire burning inside
daring me to let it loose
Instead I sit and listen
already seeing the impossibilities
already watching the ship sail
but not wanting to knock the
legs out of a man's dream
not wanting to acknowledge
that the guilt lies with me
I wonder then if he has
the same thought I do
why can't I be more like my sister

who is perfectly content to stay home
and raise her children
or maybe he is thinking
somewhere in the back of his mind
that he is glad he married me
he is glad we have all these children
he is glad to trade music
for this

The ghosts and monsters within
come out to play tonight
and they win

You Can Never Know

The air is wet and heavy, as if rain might hide in the looming clouds that blot out the sun, but
>YOU CAN NEVER KNOW

How they play in spite of what may or may not be coming, as if they have not a care in the world, and how I wish I could be like them, oblivious to
>WHAT MAY BE COMING—

What might be asked of me. I had a dream last night, and it was a good one, but the good dreams never become what is
>A LIFE OF GOOD AND PLENTY

Only the bad dreams seem like believable realities, because they are more deserved, perhaps. A black eye here, a deep wound back there, a damaged mind all around, they point to a shattered constitution.
>OR A LIFE OF ANXIOUS WONDER AND EXTRAORDINARY TRANSFORMATION

And on any given day I don't know which is better—the poetry of a disjointed life or the straight and narrow line that fragments in its own way, but on a good day, a more contemplative day,
>I KNOW WHICH I'D CHOOSE

Regret

Regret is like
an oversized rock
molded to the shoulders
of the one who is trying
to climb uphill, to a
better plane of being.
There is no point in regret,
but that doesn't mean
it does not visit us all
in the measure we allow.
We look back, and there is
always something we regret—
I should have spent
more time with my children,
I should have enjoyed more
those early unencumbered
years with my husband,
I should have roped off
time for myself.

Tonight my four-year-old son and I
were looking at old pictures,
back when his father first

asked me to marry him.
Tonight I regret not rejoicing
in the enviable body I wore then.
In fifty years I will regret
not loving this body
I wear today.

Perhaps the best thing to do, then,
is to make it a rule of life
to never regret or look back
in such a way that wishes
you could change something.
Let the past lie, and, with it,
regret.

Four-Letter Words

Let's talk about the four-letter word.
Girl
Left
Miss
Take
Wait
Dead
Slip
Fall
Tear
Talk
Feel
Hide
Fake
Deep
Dark
Mind
Gone
Pill
Live
Hope
Stay
Which of the four-letter words do you want?

Adventure

I hate getting older, I tell him.
I'm coming up on another birthday,
and birthdays always feel hard.
It's not that I'm old, really,
but I notice the aging parts now—
lines around my eyes,
puffiness around my chin,
gray hairs silvering in places.
Maybe I feel older than I really am
because it's been a hard life.
A life that has passed me by at times—
I haven't been as consciously
living it as I would like.
This life has been mostly good
but also mostly hard.
I've always wanted to rise above
where I came from,
but each passing year
leads me to believe that perhaps
I have not, perhaps I never will.
Is it too late to become
what I might have been?

Where is my sense of adventure?
I have lost it in the years
unfolding between or
perhaps I never had it.
When I was a child, adventure
meant moving from town to town,
starting over in a new place
with a new set of friends,
looking for who I was in them,
looking for the adventure
that always seemed to elude me.
My friends were the ones who
got to go on trips and explore,
but my family did not have
money to do these kinds of things.
Other people got to have
adventures, learn new things,
be different people,
but not me. Or so I thought.

The years have changed
my body and face; they have
also changed my mind.
I know two things for sure:
it is never too late to become

who you want to be and
adventure lives inside a person,
no matter the state
of their exterior world.

The Words

It is the words that stay
long after the faces have faded;
the words are the treasures,
of such great worth that
when used poorly they do not
simply fade into a background
but stand like sentries
at the entrance to a heart,
beating out all other words
intended for good

Grow a thicker skin, they said,
but, alas, I cannot. This is me,
the thinnest skin around,
everything sinking in like it
holds the key to me, or, rather,
locks the truth in a dark dungeon

And so it is not easy to simply
grow a thicker skin
How does one do such a thing?
How does one put on dismissal,
become someone they were not

only moments before,
ignore the ones who slash and scrape?

They say they cannot
teach me anything,
that the words must be
burned in a blaze,
but this, too, is not so easy
The words are my blaze
burning away my pieces,
charring sacred spaces,
consuming who I was

But perhaps this is not
so awful a purpose at all
It is only in the burning
that one rises from the ashes
in a splendid newness,
with a stronger construction,
as a more secure human being

And so
I let
them
burn

Bad Decisions

Don't do this,
don't do that,
oh, but make sure
you take care of this thing
and then you'll really
be living

A head can spin in a
billion different directions
with all the advice
that comes at a person
from every side

Well, all I know
is I'm glad I'm not that great
at listening to advice
I can't help but think
that's a good thing,
because all the bad decisions
I've ever made have
become my most valuable
learning opportunities

Ship

It bobs on water,
far beyond the realm
of imagination and yet
we see it when our eyes
flutter closed.
This ship.

It is well traveled,
well worn, perhaps,
having been tossed
amidst the stormy waters.
It is strong and quick,
slicing through calm,
carrying the hope of
every man who has
looked on it from a distance.

There they stand,
on a crowded shore,
and this ship, with its
knobby masts and
its pitching deck and
its ghost crew worn out

from the imaginary journey,
creeps closer and yet
not close enough to know
that the promises standing on deck
are nothing more than mist.

Perhaps it will get better,
perhaps it will come easier,
perhaps there are riches at the
end of the rainbow after all,
but this is not a ship
that will ever come in
and moving toward its sails
will not change its trajectory.

And so, what this ship tells us,
what it is speaking on the wind
that smacks its canvas across wood,
is do for yourselves
what a ship could never
do for you.

In Pursuit of Wisdom

The words of my youth
contain unknown wisdom,
for a heart that knows pain
can speak a true song
and yet it is years
that do the teaching

We can read all the books
and study all the lectures and
try to see through to the
very essence of a thing,
but if we have not the
life experience to make it
something more than a
cloudy haze, then we speak
of what we do not know
and our words hang empty

Wisdom, you see,
is forged in the fire
of life lived,
of lessons learned,
of time tearing

and then, wondrously,
stitching back together

Watching the Rain

It steals in
when they least
expect it

Not a cloud in the sky
and then,
the rain

They take cover inside
and they stand with their faces
pressed against a window,
noses flat, lips spread,
cheeks white against glass,
wondering, in their
silent, hopeful way,
when the downpour will stop,
when the ground will dry,
when they will be released
from the confines of
this house

They watch, mesmerized,
drops collecting in a pattern

they trace from the other side,
their fingerprints smudging
a mark that will remain
long after the rain
is gone

She pats
their heads
The best thing to do, she says,
is to let it rain
Let it wash clear
your world

Let it wash clean
the entire world

It will take many more
years for them
to understand

Thoughts on Art

I just don't like wasting time, he says,
but is anything truly wasted,
or does it all simply fall
into the file of our memory,
to leak out our fingers
the next time we pick up
a pen and try to confront
an empty page? I believe
there is nothing wasted,
because each project we complete
is only moving us closer to where
we want to be, laying the groundwork
for something even better,
offering us an opportunity
for improvement.
We can all use that.

When does the experience
become expertise,
where art takes control
and whispers those promises
about who we might be if
we continue pressing on?

Or are we mistaken,
listening to lies characteristic
of the "idealistic" generation?

She's impressed with
my process, she says.
I'd make a dream client,
or she implies it with
so many words, and then
it's my turn to flee,
because it's the thrill of the chase
that yawns before me and
pulls me back to searching.

I try not to care what they want,
because I think it's important
to stay true to what you love
and what you aspire to do,
to chase your own sort of forever
and remain open to what
may come along the way,
persevering always.

Life is a series of rushing forwards
and standing still.

You never really know
when to take the next step—
but wild race or waiting room,
each step boosts you along
to the next great thing,
which is always
on its way.

The Bottom of the World

You'll take for granted
that life is mostly good.
I mean, there are the responsibilities
nearly choking you and
activities that make your head spin
and decisions that can't really
be put off any longer,
but, for the most part, you're happy.
And then something rips the fabric,
opens you up and cleans out all your insides,
something bad, unspeakably so,
and you feel the ground you're standing on
open wide into a chasm of unknown.
You falter, rage, shake,
but none of that can close
the chasm that has been rent
in the mostly smooth silk
of your life thus far.
And you will work it,
pick at it, think on it endlessly,
until the single small rip becomes
such a gaping tear that you wonder
how they will ever put you

back together again.
You will never be able to cast
through life in the same easy way,
because the world is completely changed.
You have seen its bleak emptiness,
its terrible madness,
its frightening possibilities.
How do you live at the
bottom of the world?
Life is too hard,
too unpredictable.
You know this,
but you also cannot rid yourself
of the need to know
what happens next,
and this is why you put
one foot in front of the other,
onward, out of the dark and
into a more dangerous,
more troubled, more
wondrous world.
It is the darkness
that sharpens the colors
of the world we rediscover
in the light.

The Stranger

I watch them walking
from their cars,
not quite touching,
talking in quiet murmurs,
friends, perhaps,
but not lovers,
and then something else
catches my eye.
Two brothers on their
way in, laughing,
thumping one another
on the back, come to get
a gift for their mother or
a new book to read or
a cup of coffee together.
And off in the distance is a
little girl holding her mother's hand
across the crowded lot,
until the safety of the sidewalk.

They all live their separate lives,
lives I can only imagine,
lives that are, in their own way,

fulfilling, though they
look different.
They are oblivious to the interest
they have sparked in a stranger,
unaware that they are,
in their ordinary manner,
fascinating to watch.

Remember

You can see it in their eyes
when understanding moves
when a word hits
in just the right spot
and they don't realize that
they have known it all along
that their knowledge is carried
in their deepest places
that there is nothing
I can teach that is
worth more than
I can uncover

And so I peel it away
piece by piece
so that eyes may see
and minds may
remember

A Thousand Distractions

A thousand
shiny distractions
in a world of screens
How does one compete
with a thousand
beautiful women
on the television screen
and a thousand
stimulating conversations
on social media
and a thousand
pleasures uploaded
every second?

Closed in our bedrooms,
trapped in our cars,
walking down the street,
we are connected to screens
They are in our hands,
they are strapped to our ears,
they are locking our eyes
so we cannot hear, feel, see
the beauty unfolding around us

and maybe it's good,
because we know so much
more than we once did,
but maybe it's not,
because we don't know
much about each other now,
and which is the better life:
knowing things or
knowing people?

Who can survive
feeling forgotten?

Perhaps we were not made
for a thousand shiny distractions,
perhaps we were made
for an arm around a shoulder,
an ear tuned to a voice,
eyes locked with another

Let us not forget
each other

Naming

i

Spindly legs running
brown eyes flashing in anger,
hope, love. He is Gift.

ii

Words, valor, life, they're
his strong suit. He's unafraid.
I call him Wonder.

iii

Daring, wild one
who risks at every turn, yet
won't quit. He's Courage.

iv

Attitude, he shows
it at every turn, strong-willed,
secure. He is Love.

v

Friends found in every
stranger, he shines his light of

words. He is Kindness.

vi
Open grin, wide eyes,
contagious laughter, smiles,
dancing. He is Joy.

The Best Thing You Can Know

People ask me all the time:
What's the point of
telling that story?
It's so personal,
can't be universal.

I tell them everything
is universal, because
we find ourselves in each other.
So while I'm writing
a story about all the hell
miscarriage wrought in the
life of my family,
someone else has sunk
to the bottom of
her own despair.
She finds herself,
her survival,
her solidarity
in my story.

So I share it all.

Because the best thing
you can know in life
is that you're
not alone.
Ever.

The Difference Between Truth and Lie

You sure talk some pretty words—
your insistence that I'm beautiful—
that I'm good enough just the way I am—
that I'm a unique piece of art
you take in with hungry eyes—
and yet I've seen the way you
look at me when I've had a
bad day and I reach
for the chocolate.

You sure tell a gripping story—
about how you really want to
stop spending so much time
looking and interacting with
your fascinating phone screen—
how you want to be more present
in the small moments—
but then the next minute
I'm telling you about
something important to me—
and you've already got your phone out—
you're sending a social media message
to all your friends about how

you're going to make this change—
turn over a new leaf—
be someone better—
a study in irony at its finest.

You sure sing a pretty song—
about how my work is
important to the world—
how it doesn't matter that
it doesn't make money yet—
that you want to make sure
I still have the time needed to grow
something as important as this—
and then you're late coming home
when it's my turn to work—
and you take your time because
you don't want to be rude or
hurt someone's feelings—
and I sit at home, seething—
because it's really easy to talk the talk—
but it's not so easy to walk the walk—
and baby—that's the difference
between truth and lie—
it isn't found in the words—
it's found in the action.

This Mask

This mask is heavy,
thick, uncompromising
but it keeps me safe,
contained, insulated.
It offers me a
barrier of protection
when they ask how I'm doing
and I'd rather not say.
I smile, pat my little ones
on the head, say I'm doing
just fine, thank you,
turn the question
around to them.
And of course they're
doing just fine,
couldn't really be better,
isn't life wonderful?

This mask is large and pretentious,
covering up the skin
that twitches when
I think about what day it is
and how much I lost

on a day like this one,
but this mask conceals the loss
thoroughly and efficiently
so I look the very picture
of health and happiness and
wholehearted mother, wife,
daughter, sister,
friend.

This mask is cheap
and cracked and
wearing thin,
because outside
my son's classroom,
she says he's excelling
in first grade, don't worry,
is there something else
on my mind, why am I crying,
and the words scramble
to the back of my throat.
I want to tell her,
I need to tell her,
I'm completely alone
in what I know,
and I'm tired of pretending,

tired of hiding,
tired of the veil
between imaginary and real
when what I really want
is to be known, understood,
welcomed.
The opening widens
so dramatically I
almost walk through it.
But at the last minute,
I pull back,
for reasons
I can't say.

It's time to go,
so I rearrange this mask
and turn back down
the hall.

The Inner Chains

More than one hundred thousand kids are stolen and forced into sex slavery every year, held hostage by exploitation, greed, desire. A portion of them are rescued, and when they are cleaned up, counseled, invited back into life, they have a hard time transitioning out of trauma, because slavery runs deep.

The inner chains are the hardest to break.

A Personality Study

I like chocolate—especially the kind that's forbidden on a thirty-three-day cleanse: I dislike beets, even though I'll chop them up and juice them anyway.

I like literature written for children, though I am decidedly no longer a child: I dislike long wordy works for adults that inevitably put me to sleep.

I like movies that make me laugh but also have heart: I dislike violent films that rely on the exposure of a woman's naked body at some point during the course of the story to really sell it.

I like washing dishes after a hearty, satisfying meal: I dislike sweeping all the dropped food off the floor.

I like goodnight kisses that tell me I'll finally have a little time to myself: I dislike one more knock on the door.

I like the covers turned down and still cool to the touch, then pulled up to right under my chin in the moments before sleep: I dislike anything obstructing my face, which sends me into immediate, pervasive panic that I'm suffocating.

I like soft lighting at the end of a day, a gentle ray of consciousness: I dislike fluorescent beams ramming against my brow bone.

I like rainy days, curled up on an armchair with a book open on my lap: I dislike a stifling summer day with no shade to be found.

I like cool mountains: I dislike blistering beaches.

I like the quiet of early morning, stretching endless hours before me: I dislike the rush of an evening to meet curfew, even if it is a self-imposed one.

I like the lilting music of laughter, the gentle cadence of conversation: I dislike the jarring nature of conflict.

I like the toothpaste squeezed from the top of the tube: I dislike an empty bottom.

I like smiling at a small group of friends gathered in my living room: I dislike large parties of people I barely know.

I like handwritten notes left in the most unlikely of places: I dislike most manufactured cards.

I like genuine honesty, open hearts, and trust: I dislike sneaking, lying, and trying to hide beneath a facade.

I like working hard for something I believe in: I dislike waiting for it to pay off.

Normal

It makes you feel
different, you say.
Well, that's okay,
everybody's different
in their own way, she says.
She doesn't understand.

It makes you feel
lonely, you say.
Well, she says.
Everybody feels lonely
once in a while—
it doesn't mean you are.
She doesn't understand.

It makes you feel
angry enough to put a
hole in the wall, you say.
That's okay, she says.
Everybody gets carried
away sometimes. We'll patch it.
She doesn't understand.

It makes you feel
like a cloud is lying in wait
to ambush you, you say.
You know what? she says.
Sometimes we all feel
like there's an end to the
goodness. We only get
what we can handle.
She doesn't understand.

It makes you feel
like a day could nearly
burst with all its
goodness and light, you say.
Well, that's something, she says.
Better. Happier. Promising.
She doesn't understand.

It makes you feel
crazy, you say, all these
thoughts and emotions
at war inside, the weight
bending your back,
the urge to sleep, cut, die.
Everybody's emotions

come and go, she says.
You're all right today, aren't you?
She doesn't understand.

It makes me feel
like something is
wrong with me, you say.
Wrong in the places
you can't see, which will
soon be the places you can see—
scars and slashes
like torture souvenirs.
There's nothing wrong
with you, she says.
Nothing at all.
You're perfectly normal.

She wants so desperately
for it to be true
she wills herself
not to understand.

The Good Sense

Once I heard two boys
talking about their mother,
using shocking language
and poking fun.
They could not have been
older than eleven.

Once I saw three boys
hop a fence into a park
that was closed to all
but residents and then
bounce their basketballs
on the court with nonchalant ease,
as though they'd done
nothing wrong.
They could not have been
older than thirteen.

Once I knew five boys
who sat out by old grain dryers,
smoking their good stuff
and sipping from beer cans
they'd paid an older friend

to buy from the local
convenience store.
They could not have been
older than sixteen.

Once I felt four boys
watching me as I closed
and locked the doors
of the corner store and
ducked into my car,
hoping it would start
on the first try,
because I wouldn't know
what to do if they came for me.
They couldn't have been
older than nineteen.

Once I saw a boy
knock his fist into
another boy's jaw
and call himself
the king of the world,
so watch out, sucker.
He couldn't have been
older than twenty-three.

Once I watched six boys
romping around
in a home library
but stilling, for a moment,
for stories, and
I could not help
but wonder who
they might be grown—
and hope they had
the good sense
to choose something
better.

Life's Waxed Floors

I had been racing
around a corner too fast,
and someone had just
waxed the floor,
and you have to understand
that everything had been
flying apart at the seams,
we didn't know when
things would stabilize,
and the lighting was off,
and I was running
from something,
maybe bullies,
I don't remember,
I just remember
I took that turn
way too fast and
the floor was too slippery
and my feet flew out
from under me and
I went careening off
toward the tile floor,
and I hit hard,

I mean really hard,
it's a wonder I didn't
break something
(maybe I did),
and the whole cafeteria
grew hushed and still,
like someone had pressed
a pause button,
everyone looking at me,
waiting to see what I'd do,
and I didn't think I had
the courage or the strength
to get back up,
but I did,
so I did,
I got back up,
and I was thirty pounds lighter
and dying of an eating disorder
because life's waxed floors
are shined to
kill you.

Enlightenment vs. Hypocrisy

We are studies
in hypocrisy.
It is human nature,
the way of things.
We become comfortable
in and with our
duplicitous lives,
and so we will remain,
until we recognize
our blindness,
until we come up against
something or someone
who challenges
that blindness,
until we are willing to disclose
the holes that are in us,
the holes that are in all people.

I may be unjust,
but I labor for justice.
Perhaps I have done
unkind things, but
I am ever reaching

for kindness.
At times I may
find love difficult,
but I believe life
should be lived in
radical love.
Though I may be blind,
I rebuke my blindness.

Enlightenment diminishes
hypocrisy.

I Don't Know

"I don't know."

These are words
we don't hear
all that often now.
We fill the void
between a question
with fabrications of
our own intelligence,
because we fear
being seen as
incompetent,
idiotic,
uneducated.
We share our
guesses with authority
because the only way
people will follow us
is if we have all
the answers.

But when you ask me
if I can do this anymore,

when you ask me
how to do it anymore,
when you ask me
should I do this anymore,
the one thought
that muscles past
all the others is:
I don't know.

Woman

You will never understand me.
What brings me pleasure today
may not bring me pleasure
tomorrow.
The explanation I give you
for my silence today may not be
what explains my silence
tomorrow.
The possibilities I consider today
may not seem like possibilities
tomorrow.

You will think you know me
inside out today, but I will
show you someone different
tomorrow.

I am a woman—
made to be loved,
not understood.

Poverty

There is more than
poverty of circumstance.
There is poverty of mind,
poverty of spirit,
poverty of emotional stability,
and it is here that I find myself
stumbling over the sharp edge of unreason.
It is here, in this poverty,
that the well being of mind,
the heartiness of spirit,
the meaning of stability
wavers, topples, comes undone.

It is undone.
I am undone.

And before me stands
a person I might never have
imagined could be me,
but, then, it is difficult to know
what one might become
in poverty.
It is difficult to know

what one might do
or say or begin to believe
until the emptiness yawns
before an overwhelmed heart
and it's do or die,
according to desperation,
and it's sink or swim,
according to survival,
and it's choose or be chosen,
according to the order of the day.

So which will it be?
Virtuous or impious?
Gentle or cruel?
Smooth water or volcanic lands?

Well, one can never know
what one might become
in poverty.

Solidarity

The air is light,
sustaining a whole world.
Free.

Sunlight splashes the walk
where she sets her feet,
and I fall in beside her.
It is but a few moments
spent in silence before
the world begins to crack open
around the edges in a
gentle yet profound way.

I don't know how you do it, she says.
And what she's really saying,
underneath the words,
in the place where one must
listen with the heart
rather than the ears,
is *I don't know how to do it*.

So, rather than say
what it is I do,

what it is, exactly,
that she should do,
what it is that would make
all her problems set like
the sun's last rays,
I tell her the truth.

I don't do it.
Not even close.
I tell her because
what I desire,
at the very heart of me,
is to disrobe, to unlock
all the sacred doors,
to fling away this
jagged weight of pretense
so that others may find courage
to walk bare and unadorned.

She smiles and dips her head
and whispers, *Okay*.
But there is more, too, to this,
more that hides on the
underside of words,
more that clings with claws

that will pull her through
the next year of days
or longer, if she's lucky,
more that is, perhaps,
the very meaning of life.

A heart that feels
it is not alone
is a heart that becomes
like the air:
Light,
sustaining a whole world.
Free.

Found

Another shooting today.
This one took fifty,
injured fifty-three.

One man did it.
One man who thought
he needed to cleanse the world
of a population he hated,
walked into a night club,
opened fire,
watched the bodies fall.
Three hours he was there,
doing God knows what,
saying God knows what—
unspeakable things,
or nothing at all?

He's not the first, of course.
There have been others—
opening fire in movie theaters,
elementary schools,
inside an Amish schoolhouse.
He won't be the last.

It's always a shattering day
when it happens.
We are shaken from
our sense of safety,
from our seemingly
impenetrable veneers,
from our comfortable lives
by this uncomfortable knowing
that it could have been us
or our children or our
mothers, fathers, sisters, brothers,
friends, business partners,
yoga instructors, flight attendants,
nannies, grocery store clerks,
lawyers, judges, schoolteachers,
the Internet star we watched
on a YouTube rise to fame.
Death is always jolting
in its unexpected shattering.

And every time it happens
I wonder, what does it take
to get a person to that point,
what would it require to snap a mind

and walk a man inside a door
to murder innocent people?
What kind of life,
past, present, future
drives him, her, us,
to a place of unreason,
a place of mental derangement,
a place where a world without
these particular people—
men, women, children—
would be a better world?
Could he have been me?
Could he have been you?
Will he be my son, my friend,
my colleague, a man
I pass one day on the street?

We all contain the capacity
for goodness and evil
in somewhat equal measure.
But despite everything—
despite even this—
I believe that people are good
in the deepest places
of their hearts.

Some of us lose ourselves
along our traveling way,
because life burns and
tears and splits.
But we are never so far
from our truest selves
that we cannot again
be found.

A Life Lived

There is a place where
the walls are not so high,
where they are nothing more than
small, insignificant hurdles,
opaque and thin,
that would not require
much time to climb and
peer at what lies inside.

And there is another place
where the walls stand
thick and high and wide
and one could not hope
to scale their magnificence
nor touch their icy smooth
nor try to see through them
at the very least.

Walls such as these
are not meant to yield.
They are walls built of fear,
of disappointment, of all
we do not understand.

They are walls that divide
and separate and condemn,
and they build more walls
every time their strength is tested,
and before we know it,
this place of walls reaching
to the heights and plunging
to the depths is the place
our hearts reside.

And a wall
does not open.

A life lived within a wall
does not open.
A life lived within a wall
is a lonely one.

A life lived
within a wall
needs a hole
where a bridge can hang,
where a bridge can connect,
where a bridge can open.

The End

About the Author

Rachel is the author of three poetry books, *This is How You Know*, *Life: a definition of terms*, and *The Book of Uncommon Hours*, and a middle grade novel in verse, *The Colors of the Rain*. She has been writing poetry since the time she could hold a pencil and form what passed for letters on the page. Her first introduction to poetry was the brilliance of Shel Silverstein, whom she still reads today. She recently exposed her sons to the hilarious Jack Prelutsky poem, "Homework! Oh Homework!" which was one of her favorites as a kid. They loved it (as she still does).

Her poems for children and adults can be read in literary magazines and online publications around the world.

Rachel lives with her husband and six sons in San Antonio, Texas. She daily reads poetry (as well as many, many books) to her children, because poetry, she says, contains the essence of life, and reading, she says, is the gateway to a future of promise.

Author's Note

My dear reader,

I hope that in the pages of this book, you have found bits and pieces of yourself, bits and pieces of truth, and bits and pieces of hope. I hope you have seen, in some small way, that our bits and pieces, the sum of our parts, all the subjects and separate compartments that make up the whole of us, are remarkably beautiful and most of all: worthy. And I hope that you will be encouraged and bolstered to live your fullest life—all parts considered.

In love,
Rachel

Acknowledgments

My poetry is penned in the most solitary of places (though sometimes one of my sons barges in to say hello; I don't usually mind), but it is not a solitary effort that puts its finished form into your hands. I am indebted to:

Ben: As always, your encouragement means the world to me. Your book covers are some of my favorite pieces of art. Thank you for supporting this dream, for guiding me back to the path when I get sidetracked, and for believing in me even when my belief is shaken. You are my sunshine (I mean that in the cheesiest way).

Jadon, Asa, Hosea, Zadok, Boaz, and Asher: Your laughter sounds like poetry to me. Your voices, too. And the shape of your love is a poem. I do not have to work all that hard to take these moments with which you gift me and fashion them into poetry. I love you so very, very much.

Cathy Merwarth: Thank you for your constant love and encouragement.

Mom: Thank you for stocking your library with my books and for telling everyone we meet that I'm an author and I have books, do you want to buy one? Your support has always been life-giving.

My readers: Thank you for paying attention and for continuing to read.

My extended family: Thank you for giving me these stories and poems to write and share. I am also a sum of you.

Enjoy more poetry from Rachel Toalson

racheltoalson.com/poetry

Rachel Toalson Poetry
Starter Library

Enjoy more of Rachel Toalson's poetry with these free downloads.

To get your FREE books, visit *
RachelToalson.com/FreeBook

*Must be 13 or older to be eligible

www.ingramcontent.com/pod-product-compliance
Lightning Source LLC
Chambersburg PA
CBHW020122130526
44591CB00032B/320